Inua Ellams, after Sophocles

methuen | drama

LONDON • NEW YORK • OXFORD • NEW DELHI • SYDNEY

METHUEN DRAMA
Bloomsbury Publishing Plc
50 Bedford Square, London, WC1B 3DP, UK
1385 Broadway, New York, NY 10018, USA
29 Earlsfort Terrace, Dublin 2, Ireland

BLOOMSBURY, METHUEN DRAMA and the Methuen
Drama logo are trademarks of Bloomsbury Publishing Plc

First published in Great Britain 2022

This edition published 2023

A catalogue record for this book is available from the British Library.

A catalog record for this book is available from the Library of Congress

ISBN: PB: 978-1-3504-3013-6
ePDF: 978-1-3504-3014-3
eBook: 978-1-3504-3015-0

Series: Modern Plays

Typeset by Mark Heslington Ltd, Scarborough, North Yorkshire
Printed and bound in Great Britain

To find out more about our authors and books visit
www.bloomsbury.com and sign up for our newsletters.

Antigone was commissioned by and first performed at Regent's Park Open Air Theatre, London, on 9 September 2022 with the following cast and crew:

Antigone	**Zainab Hasan**
Eurydice	**Pandora Colin**
Lyra	**Rhianna Dorris**
Aleksy	**Sandy Grierson**
Ismene	**Shazia Nicholls**
Polyneices	**Nadeem Islam**
Eteocles	**Abe Jarman**
Creon	**Tony Jayawardena**
Haemon	**Oliver Johnstone**
Nikomedes/Cover Creon	**Munir Khairdin**
Commissioner	**Susan Lawson-Reynolds**
Tiresius	**Eli London**
Cover Polyneices and Eteocles/ Chorus/Dance Captain	**Mervin Noronha**
Athan	**Razak Osman**
Officer	**Joseph Prouse**
Kyria	**Nadia Sohawon**
Strom	**Riley Woodford**

Composer   Michael 'Mikey J' Asante MBE
Casting Assistant   Shanaé Chisholm
Voice & Text and Season Associate Director   Barbara Houseman
Choreographer   Carrie-Anne Ingrouille
Casting Director   Polly Jerrold
Lighting Designer   Jack Knowles
Sound Designer   Emma Laxton
Season Associate: Intimacy Support   Ingrid Mackinnon
Costume Designer   Khadija Raza
Set Designer   Leslie Travers
Co-Director   Jo Tyabaji
Dramaturg   Nic Wass
Fight Director   Kate Waters
Director   Max Webster
Costume Supervisor   Lisa Aitken
Company Stage Manager   Jo Alexander

Production Manager   Andy Beardmore
Deputy Stage Manager   Amy Bending
Assistant Stage Manager   Ana Carter
Props Supervisor   Lizzie Frankl for Propworks
Associate Props Supervisor   Poppy Morris for Propworks

Acknowledgements

In chronological order, thanks to:

Max Webster, Tim Sheader, Nic Wass, Jo Tyabji, Suhaiyma Manzoor-Khan, Yasmin Abdel-Magied, Namsi Khan, H.R.H. Prince Ghazi Bin Muhammad, Joelle Taylor, Lucy Webster, Anjuli Bedi, Raina Hafez, Alia Bano, Michael 'Mikey J' Asante, Shanaé Chisholm, Barbara Houseman, Carrie-Anne Ingrouille, Polly Jerrold, Jack Knowles, Emma Laxton, Ingrid Mackinnon, Khadija Raza, Leslie Travers, Kate Waters, Pandora Colin, Rhianna Dorris, Sandy Grierson, Zainab Hasan, Nadeem Islam, Abe Jarman, Tony Jayawardena, Oliver Johnstone, Munir Khairdin, Susan Lawson-Reynolds, Eli London, Shazia Nicholls, Mervin Noronha, Razak Osman, Joseph Prouse, Nadia Sohawon, Riley Woodford, Lydia Bakelmun.

Antigone's response in Act Two beginning 'This is my freckled forehead' is a poem originally commissioned by the English and Media Centre and published in *The Facility and Other Texts – Re-imagining Antigone* (2022). It is reproduced as part of this play with kind permission of the Centre.

https://www.englishandmedia.co.uk/publications/the-facility-and-other-texts-antigone-re-imagined-emc-cultural-conversation

Antigone

Cast

Antigone, *younger niece of* **Creon**
Creon, *Prime Minister*
Aleksy, *Senior Political Aide*
Ismene, *older niece of* **Creon**, *Political Aide*
Haemon, **Antigone**'s *fiancée and* **Creon**'s *step son*
Eurydice, *wife of* **Creon**
Nikomedes, *Imam*
Commissioner, *Commissioner of Police*
Eteocles, *older brother of* **Antigone** *and* **Ismene**
Polyneices, *younger brother of* **Antigone** *and* **Ismene**
Tiresias, *computer data expert*
Bodyguard, *always at* **Tiresias'** *side*
Officer, *Metropolitan Police Officer*
Reporter, *news reporter*
Athan, *member of youth group and friend of* **Polyneices**
Strom, *member of youth group and friend of* **Polyneices**
Kyria, *friend of* **Antigone** *and Parliamentary Assistant*
Lyra, *friend of* **Antigone**
Chorus, *the Citizens*

Act One

Scene One

The Queen Elizabeth Youth Centre is throwing a closing-down party. People hold banners saying 'Q.E. 4 Eva', 'Never Forget', 'Closing Down but Staying Strong'.

The cast dance the electric slide with **Antigone** *at the centre, beside* **Athan***. Upstage,* **Polyneices** *and* **Strom** *play video games.*

When the song finishes, they applaud the DJ, until **Antigone** *calls them to attention. They sit or crouch as she performs a poem assisted by* **Kyria** *and* **Lyra***.*

Antigone
You are my people
and I find you in the streets and shadows,
in the wild and hollowed out hills of this city,
this hungry country, this hulking mass.

You with the sari and bindi like a moon
on your forehead are my people

You with the blazer of pins and badges
like chain mail stitched to fabric are my people

You who always prays are my people
you who never prays are my people

You with the flat cap and carton of juice
you who always stops quarrels for truce

You who always starts battles, who boos
at everything you are my people

You who brings extra lunch for who needs,
you who always needs, you are my people

You in the kurta and you in flip flops,
you in trainers and you in your socks

You who is bejewelled and you without any,
you in the hijab and you with out any
you are my people, you are my plenty

you of broken homes and empty houses
you of full houses but no one to hold,
you are my people, you are my home

and even as the government who funded our walls
retracts their funding to watch our walls fall
you are my people, you are my all

you are my night's moon, my morning's sun
my afternoon's breeze, my evening's calm

my past, my present, my guiding song
towards the future and what lies beyond

You are my people, you are my people,
you are my backbone, you are my hugs

my bruvs, my sisters, my peace, my olive branch,
my leaves, my doves, my loves . . .

let this day mark an era,
let's celebrate our years together

and promise, come hailstones, sandstorm or thunder
we be our people, there for each other.

Chorus We be our people, there for each other.

They applaud **Antigone**, *embracing each other. Music starts. They break into smaller groups.* **Polyneices** *and* **Strom** *resume their game as* **Athan** *totters towards them, tipsy and happy.*

Athan P, your sister's actually dope. Like, actually.

Polyneices Ew.

Athan Not like that! Can't believe this place is closing.

Strom Ask your uncle to do something.

Polyneices You ask him.

Athan (*laughs*)   Want us to roll up on the Home Secretary?

Strom *laughs.*

Athan   Here.

Athan *offers him a beer.*

Polyneices   I'm driving.

Athan   It's a video game, bruv.

Strom (*laughs*)   You're in an army truck! Take it.

Polyneices   I don't drink.

Strom   Since when?!

Strom *shoots someone in the game.*

Polyneices   Oi! You're supposed to shoot guys shooting us!

Strom *shoots more.*

Polyneices   Those are our guys!

Strom   Can't tell the difference, mate. The bad guys look exactly the same with towels on their heads.

Athan *laughs.*

Athan *accidentally spills the drink on* **Polyneices**.

Polyneices   Athan, what you doing?! And Strom man, can't tell the difference, don't play.

Strom   It's not real life.

Polyneices   You'll know the difference in real life?

Athan   Shussssh man! Just play!

They play on.

Antigone, *wading through the party, spots* **Lyra** *and* **Kyria** *lighting a spliff.*

Antigone   Is that you, yeah? Pass it then.

Lyra *passes it over,* **Antigone** *takes a long drag and holds it in.*
Kyria *stares in awe.*

Kyria   How does she hold it in for so long?

Antigone   Training fam, training. Lots of practice.

Lyra *(laughs)*   Isn't this haram?

Antigone   We been bunning for years. Now you ask?

Lyra   Is it?

Antigone   Technically, yes, but the Sufis, the mystic hippy
Muslims in old Pakistan, said it detaches the spirit from
earthly troubles, elevating one's consciousness.

Kyria   Right, right.

Antigone   I'm serious. The Qualandars, my ancestors did
that. Then colonisation, Victorians came, killed a bunch of
them, outlawed the practice, but yeah. Bunning's in my
blood.

Lyra *and* **Kyria** *laugh.*

Antigone   Anyway, I need to chill and not get emotional
about all this.

Kyria   You did everything you could. Camped outside the
council for how many weeks?

Lyra   Everyone knows you've loved this place since the day
your mum dropped you lot off. This is not your fault. Best
youth leader by far.

Antigone   It's them I'm worried about. Where're they
gonna go? Where're you gonna go?

Kyria   I'm gonna chat to your sister about her internship.
Why don't you do it?

Antigone   Kyria, I hate politics. Rather work with real
people.

Kyria   Where's your sister anyway?

Ismene *enters with* **Haemon**.

Haemon   I can see why this means so much to Antigone.

Ismene   It's meant a lot to all of us.

Haemon   Shame it's shutting down.

Lyra   She's just walked in. Who's the cute white boy she's with? Keeps staring at you.

Antigone *waves at* **Haemon**, *who waves back.*

Antigone   We're kinda . . . living together.

Kyria   You what?

Antigone (*laughs*)   He's my uncle's step son, Haemon, just back from uni.

Lyra   Posh boys, is that you yeah?

Antigone *laughs.*

Lyra   Well, he's not looking at you like a step sister.

Antigone   Stop it! He's just being supportive.

Upstage, the quarrel heats up.

Polyneices   STROM! STOP SHOOTING THEM!

Strom   They're all rag heads. We *should* be shooting them.

Polyneices   Jesus Christ!

Athan   Nah, Muhammed.

Strom (*laughs*)   King of all rag heads.

Polyneices *leaps on* **Athan**. **Strom** *leaps on* **Polyneices**. *They fight as* **Antigone, Lyra, Kyria, Ismene** *and* **Haemon** *race to part them.* **Eteocles** *arrives to hold* **Polyneices**.

Polyneices   Call 'em rag heads again, see what happens.

Strom   They're pixels Polyneices, they don't exist.

Athan   Lucky your brother's here.

Strom   He's lost it. Bunking school, missing shifts.

Athan   Kyria saw him selling incense on the streets.

Kyria   Shut up, man!

Eteocles   This true, Nicey?

Polyneices   Least it's honest clean work.

Athan   Started wearing kaftans.

Polyneices   More comfortable than jeans.

Eteocles   If you're not family, leave!

Strom   We haven't finished the game / yet

Athan   Can't tell us what to do.

Antigone   Go. It's okay.

Athan *and* **Strom** *leave.* **Lyra** *and* **Kyria** *cross their arms and kiss their teeth, refusing to leave.*

Antigone   Guys, I'll find you later.

Lyra *and* **Kyria** *leave.*

Eteocles   You skipping school? Answer the question.

Polyneices   I . . . don't have the brains man, like Antigone, Ismene and you. It's always been tough for me. Even the teacher said I should do carpentry or plumbing. Who's gonna marry a plumber?

Eteocles   Is this about girls?

Polyneices   Are you an idiot?

Eteocles   Are you an idiot?

Antigone   Oh grow up! What's wrong with both of you!

Eteocles   We need plumbers in the city. What's incense gonna do?

Polyneices (*laughs*)   He's still a cadet, already moving like he owns the city.

Eteocles   It's fun! I work with good guys. We uphold the law.

Polyneices   You forgotten what this country did to us? Dividing India? Three wars over Kashmir? Millions killed in Pakistan, our great aunts and uncles.

Eteocles   Who we never met or spoke to.

Polyneices   So?

Eteocles   All in the past anyway.

Polyneices   Torture? Drone strikes?! They are still bombing weddings! It's all in the present.

Antigone   He's right. Then here, police, your lot, treating black or brown people as suspicious. You know how many times they've stopped him?

Eteocles   When you're not in school, you are suspicious.

Antigone   No he's not.

Polyneices   See!

Antigone   But you should be in school.

Eteocles   See!

Polyneices   Why you here? You stopped coming years ago.

Eteocles   I still care about this place.

Polyneices   Then pull some strings! Help keep it open! Defund the police to fund youth centres. This is the only place I got. Where am I gonna go?

Eteocles   I know where you go, who you hang with. They're dangerous.

Polyneices   No they're not. They just . . . understand things.

Antigone   Who? What things?

Eteocles Polyneices Lakhani, stay away from them.

Polyneices We just talk! That's all. I've so many questions, so many Muslims in refugee camps, 30 million from Palestine, Nigeria, Libya, China! We are failing all of them.

Ismene Failing Muslims? You stopped coming to mosque when Antigone did.

Antigone I still pray. Sometimes.

Polyneices Jihad means 'struggle', but does that mean prayer or war?

Antigone We can't talk about this here.

Polyneices Where then?! When? You're never around! You too, and you, Izzy.

Ismene I have to be at work. Come to mosque, we can ask Nikomedes.

Polyneices Tried that. He won't talk to me, told me to leave last time.

Eteocles Just stay away from them.

Antigone We can't police his friends, Ety.

Ismene Don't be so naïve. He keeps vanishing, running away from private security.

Polyneices They scare me man, why they following me around?

Eteocles 'Cause we're under Uncle's care and he is the HOME SECRETARY. Stay away from them.

Ismene Uncle didn't have to take us in after Mum and Dad died. Under his roof, there are certain things we can't do.

Eteocles I'm the eldest, you have to do what I say. Stop hanging with them or you're out.

Polyneices What? It's not your house.

Antigone   Uncle knows you're doing this?

Ismene   He told Ety to sort this out.

Antigone   This is wrong. If he goes, I go.

Beat.

Eteocles   So be it.

Polyneices   Fine. Never liked that fancy house anyway. And I got real brothers, who'll die for me.

Ismene   Nicey, calm down!

Polyneices   Don't touch me, man.

Polyneices *leaves.*

Antigone (*walking after him*)   POLYNEICES!

Ismene   Antigone, you need to be here!

Antigone   Damn it! Ety, fix this.

Eteocles *sighs and runs after* **Polyneices**.

Scene Two

Campaign trail, general elections.

There are banners with slogans 'Creon for PM', 'Let the caretaker take care', 'Take care', 'Vote Creon'. **Creon** *walks about shaking hands. As he does, members of the crowd become a* **Chorus**.

Chorus
These are the days of battle and brawn
when the soul of the country is scattered and torn
and the throne of power is empty and none
of the candidates clamouring is clearly the one.

You have liberals promising infinite growth
if the country's heart is always exposed
and our welcoming mat is always unrolled
to invite the needy into our homes.

Conservatives promising to close up those doors,
reinstate values, traditional ones,
replace big government's expensive claws
with an attitude quantified, measured and small.

The greens and their radical naturist plans
to label capitalist ventures as scams,
to make our kingdom a socialist land,
and ensure sustainable promises stand.

These are the days of battle and brawn
when the soul of the country is scattered and torn
and the throne of power is empty and none
of the candidates clamouring is clearly the one.

The deluge of jargon and volume of chatter
drowns the attempt to hone in on what matters
they're all as convinced as the former or latter
and blur to one bubbling babbling blather.

The battle gets darker as it goes on,
they dig through backgrounds for embarrassing bombs
to drop on each other's campaigning runs,
common decency, decorum is gone.

It pushes us towards comfortable voices,
grandfather's and mother's, their votes and choices,
the worlds they came from, victories and losses,
our confusions deepen, carts before horses.

These are the days of battle and brawn
when the soul of the country is scattered and torn
and the throne of power is empty and none
of the candidates clamouring is clearly the one.

And who wins the race, who comes number one,
is usually the loudest with the biggest drum,
a towering presence, familiar and strong
and Creon Jafari isn't the one.

Antigone *and* **Haemon**'*s flat.* **Antigone** *is with* **Lyra** *and members of the youth center.*

Ismene *calls* **Antigone**'*s phone.*

Ismene (*to* **Creon**)   You're on in five.

Antigone   What?

Ismene   Y . . . you answered?

Antigone   I'm tired. What is it?

Ismene   We are in your neighbourhood. Campaigning. And I thought . . . You should be here.

Antigone   For this vanity project? A general election? You know he's never gonna win, right?

Ismene   It'd still be nice to see you.

Antigone   Four years since Polyneices vanished. Creon has not said a word.

Ismene   Y . . . yes. You and Nicey both chose to move out.

Antigone   Chose to move out?

Ismene   Uncle didn't force either of you to leave.

Antigone   But Polyneices left because of him.

Ismene   Nicey will come back when he is ready. He is still finding himself.

Antigone   For four years?! Is he even alive?

Ismene   Of course he is! We have to have faith! We. How are you?

Antigone   Told you, tired. I work two jobs to buy food and clothes to keep these kids safe. Lyra helps, cleans my flat after . . . 'cause those kids are chaos.

Ismene   You're turning your flat into a youth centre? Nene, is that safe? If anything happens, you'd be liable. It's not your job.

Antigone   I should be a political aide like you? Running after Creon?

Ismene   I . . . saw pictures of you in the paper. You didn't look . . . If you want to do this properly, you should become a local representative. You'll have actual power / to demand

Antigone   I don't care about politics, you know this.

Ismene   You should be here. We should be together. Uncle is about to give his final campaign speech / and

Eteocles *enters hurriedly.*

Eteocles   Is that Antigone? / Is that

Ismene   The family should be together. We are close by.

Antigone   Four years. Four.

Eteocles   I have to talk to both of you.

Antigone   Is that Ety? I don't want to talk to him.

Eteocles *grabs the phone.*

Ismene   Wait / wait wait! No Ety!

Eteocles   Hello? Hello? Antigone you have to come down. Hello?!

Antigone *hangs up.*

Campaign trail; **Creon** *mounts a podium with* **Eurydice** *at his side. The crowd applauds politely. Among them:* **Nikomedes** *and* **Alkesy**.

Creon   It was a great honour to have taken care of this country's borders and laws as Home Secretary, but much of what I practised I learnt in my family's corner shop where my mother began setting us chores. My siblings and I would quarrel, the chores would go undone, until one day, Mother, too exhausted to chase after us, stuck five balloons to the notice board, balloons on which she'd drawn lovely smiley faces, took out a toothpick and popped one. The sound crushed us. 'If your chores are not complete, I will pop another', Mother said. Pretty soon we began finishing our chores, working together to take care of the balloons, and after each successful day, Mother would add a new one until the shop was overflowing with balloons, spreading joy to our customers; our shop thrived! Mother laid down the law, it brought prosperity, fairness and order to our shop. I carried this memory, its lessons of collaborative work and equal responsibility, through Law School, into politics, where I too laid fair laws to take care of our families, our borders, and take care of our country. Only when I was certain they would take care of our bright future did I accept the challenge of leading the party in this general election. Now, some of you may wonder if in a world of economic uncertainty, a care taker can help our families unite our diverse stories into one national narrative. With great humility heed my response: Yes, I can. There is no better candidate to safeguard the wishes and dreams of our Great Britain. My name is Creon Jafari and your future is safe in my hands.

The crowd cheer. **Creon** *steps down and walks among them, shaking hands.*

Eteocles' *phone rings.*

Eteocles   Hello? Who is this? Nicey?!

Ismene   What?! Is he back?

Eteocles   What?
No.
Don't do this.
Hello? Hello?!

Eteocles *hangs up.*

Eteocles   I have to go.

Ismene   What? Go where? Ety!

Eteocles   Don't tell anyone!

Eteocles *leaves.*

Creon   So, updates?

Beat.

Eurydice   It's been an incredibly well-run campaign.

Haemon   Absolutely.

Ismene   We had the best people. The best PR.

Creon   You did a phenomenal job, son.

Haemon   Easiest job, Dad. And asking to be elected to continue taking care, in a general election, is trending really well. A perfect blend of humility and aspiration.

Aleksy   Your vision is so clear, I see it and believe it.

Eurydice   You love this country. It's evident in all you say and do. The people got to see that, it's been so worthwhile.

Creon   You always know what to say.

Eurydice   I'm being honest. That's how I got the most powerful business women to donate to your campaign.

Creon   No, it's because you are a force of nature and they have to stay in your good books.

Eurydice *laughs.*

Creon   You don't think I might have appeared weak? A bit too humble?

Eurydice   There's not enough humility in politics. Your ambition has always been tempered by your modesty. That's what drew me to you in Law School, and whatever happens tonight, hold on to it, and others will be drawn to you too.

They embrace, part, and he sees her face.

Creon   It's not enough, is it?

Eurydice   No, it's not looking in our favour.

Aleksy   I have a few bold suggestions. I have here the most comprehensive data sets ever compiled of the entire electorate. From this / we can strategise a

Creon (*laughs*)   Data sets? Surely it's too late for that?

Eurydice   Only five hours left. It is too late.

Creon   Right. I thought the country was ready to get behind someone like . . . me. Well, polling stations are still filling up. Keep our volunteers positive, pounding pavements, chasing each vote. Ismene reach out to . . .?

Ismene *is looking at her tablet.*

Creon   Ismene? What's the matter? What is it?

Ismene   Live news. Polyneices. Uncle, they've found him.

They gather round **Ismene**'s *tablet.*

Antigone *and* **Haemon**'s *flat:* **Antigone**'s *phone rings.*

Lyra   Antigone?

Antigone   I don't want to speak to her and Eteocles.

Lyra   Nene /

Antigone   and if they can't see what we are doing here

Lyra   Nee /

Antigone   Then I'm not gonna support / them

Lyra   Antigone!

Lyra *passes her phone.* **Antigone** *looks at it. Across the city, mobile phones ring. At some point everyone is looking at screens. Gun shots ring out. All on stage turn away at the same time, horrified.* **Antigone** *drops the phone and screams.*

Campaign trail:

Ismene   Go to Antigone.

Haemon *leaves.*

Aleksy   This is not the end.

Creon   What?

Aleksy   Of your campaign. This is not the end.

Creon   My campaign?

Eurydice   Creon.

Aleksy   Do not let this derail your future. This is an opportunity we can work with.

Scene of the attack:

Commissioner   Several people have died and many injured in simultaneous attacks across our capital. Seven suspects drove vehicles, ploughing through pedestrians. The casualties include a police officer, run down after fatally shooting one of the suspects. This is the most devastating attack on our capital and I am declaring a state of emergency. With a heavy heart, I can now confirm the officer who died as Eteocles Lakhani, and the driver he shot dead as his own brother, Polyneices Lakhani.

Antigone *and* **Haemon***'s flat:* **Haemon** *enters.*

Haemon   Antigone?!

Antigone   Haemon.

Haemon   Don't look at it.

Antigone   Why?! Why? Why?

Haemon   I love you. I love you so much.

Campaign trail: **Aleksy** *hands* **Creon** *and* **Eurydice** *a copy of a speech.* **Creon** *glances down at papers.*

Creon   You are positive this is what the British public need to hear?

Aleksy   There's still a chance, but you have to go further. The data never lies.

Creon   The first word is terrorists . . . I can't say that. We don't know anything about their motivations. It's too soon. Eurydice?

Eurydice   I agree. We would be stirring up dangerous sentiments, it could backfire, no.

Creon   We use something else.

Aleksy   You are losing this election, Creon. This is the only way you can win.

Eurydice   'Their presence infects many parts.' No, this is horrific. This is way too far.

Creon   How can this help me win?

Aleksy   We do not have time for me to explain / the ins and outs of

Creon   Then no.

Aleksy   Okay. There are certain late-voting subsets of our electorate for whom certain terminology evokes strong reactions. We disseminate footage, clips of you using such terminology across their timelines – I'm talking targeted, specific, precise exposure, from a man of your . . . character speaking on these issues – and I guarantee it will be enough to rouse them vote, to win you this election.

Eurydice   I strongly advise against this.

Aleksy   Cometh the moment, cometh the man. This is your moment, only you can lead us now.

Creon   I . . . I don't think I can speak these words.

Aleksy   I'll help you.

Antigone *and* **Haemon**'s *flat:* **Antigone** *has been crying.*

Haemon   He won.

Antigone   What?

Haemon   Dad.

Antigone   He was losing and used Polyneices. 'Their presence infects many parts of our country'? Infects? People should be terrified of him. Why did Nicey come back? What was he thinking?

Haemon   We will never truly know.

Antigone   How could Nicey have done something like that?

Antigone *takes out her phone and begins typing.*

Haemon   Don't go trying to find out. If you're found with any kind of terro . . . unusual material, you'd be arrested. Lyra needs you, and the kids; you keep them safe. The press will hound all of you even more.

Lyra   You have to be careful. You're dating the Prime Minister's son.

Antigone   Step son!

Lyra   Doesn't matter. The plans you guys have . . . you'll lose everything.

Haemon   Ismene is here.

Ismene *enters.*

Beat.

Antigone   Both of them?

Beat.

Ismene   I know.

Beat.

Antigone   And Creon, what is he doing? How can he . . . He described us as a virus / to be disinfected

Ismene   We had nephews.

Antigone   Nephews?

Haemon   What?

Ismene   Nicey emailed Ety just before he . . . In Syria, he became a dad. His wife died and he wanted to come back with his two boys. He reached out the British authorities offering information. They brought him here, but denied his kids. They died of hunger.

Beat.

Antigone   Hunger? What were their names?

Ismene   Athan and Strom.

Lyra   After his friends from the Youth Centre.

Ismene   Yes. They were twins.

Antigone   Nicey, Ety . . . all of them, gone. Just you and me left of our family.

Ismene   They tortured him, Neenee.

Beat.

The sisters rush to embrace.

Antigone   Does Creon know all this?

Ismene   I don't think so.

Beat.

Antigone   We should ask Nikomedes to conduct their funerals.

Ismene   Yes. He's known us for ever.

Antigone   Do you have his number? We kinda fell out.

Ismene   I'll find it. Taubah astaghfirullah. I can't believe this is happening.

Chorus: *across the city.*

Chorus

There will be sunrise over the city,
it will look brighter than its ever before,
kissing all our splendid boroughs,
cutting through darkness, light will pour,
dance on the river, blades of gold,
coating the water, rippling out,
bleaching the black flags of attackers,
obliterating them, burning them back.

Polyneices brought chaos and madness
to darken our city, his voice like a knife.
Seven metal talons scratching our streets,
mowing down people, snuffing our light.
Before he could torch our homes and towers
destroy us, crush us completely,
our great city which never cowers,
rose up before him, brave, shouting Freeze!

And God, who hates braggers and violence
watched them driving, hatred in their chests
and when he'd seen and heard enough,
shot their man, took away his breath.
One moment, anger and murder on his
mind, next, dead, no fanfare no noise,
and the others hunted, cornered, destroyed.

Seven hostiles, seven boroughs,
several whole lives lost in our city.
So many wounded, many maimed
many frightened fractured families.

And though we'll cry through the night,
mornings bring cleansing light.
The blood will dry, roads will clear
we won't awake with doubts or fears
'cause this is England: we're stained with tears
but send seven more, we're staying right here,
send seven hundred, we're staying right here,
seven thousand, we're staying right here!

They cheer.

Far off, a muezzin sings the call to prayer as Muslims pray.

Scene Three

Downing Street: **Creon** *surrounded by* **Aleksy**, **Eurydice**, *aides and the* **Commissioner**. **Tiresias** *stands, watching.*

Creon   Today, the sun rises for Great Britain, but sets for terrorism. By electing me Prime Minster you, the British public have given me the mandate to effectively counter extremism. To that effect I would like to announce a . . . Three Tier Counter Threat Bill, designed to discourage and destroy terrorism, foreign and domestic. My own nephew, Polyneices Lakhani, who brought terror to our streets, is subject to this bill. His brother, Eteocles Lakhani, who died protecting our freedoms will be buried this afternoon, with the highest possible honours in the heart of our capital. I urge you to attend his funeral. But Polyneices will receive no honour in death. With immediate effect, he is stripped of British citizenship and his body will be detained indefinitely pending necessary procedures. To those who will say this infringes on his Human Rights, I am calling for a British Bill of Rights because the Human Rights Act does not serve us. Too often it allows for criminality to charge unchecked through our streets. With my intimate knowledge of the range of issues, it is clear to me this is the correct course of action. To the other perpetrators still at large, there is no place to hide, there is no place for hate here. Our country is a network of families; I am the head of all families and I will protect our families from you. You will be brought to justice. I am Creon Jafari and I will do my job.

The crowd begins to disperse, but **Tiresias** *stands, unmoving, facing* **Creon** *as he steps down.*

Aleksy   Masterful Prime Minister, strong leadership.

Eurydice   Strong leadership?

Creon   You disagree?

Eurydice   Stripping him of citizenship?

Creon   Eurydice, he killed people. He lost the privilege to be British when he attacked us.

Eurydice   Privilege?

Creon   And Pakistan can claim him if they want.

Eurydice   He can't apply for Pakistani citizenship, for any citizenship . . . that is making him stateless, you are breaking international law.

Creon   I'm not, I'm protecting our people.

Eurydice   And we used to read the Human Rights Act to each other. We'd point out some flaws, but overwhelmingly you and I agreed it served the greater good. And now . . . it does not serve us?

Creon   The British people need to feel safe and protected.

Eurydice   Which British people?

Creon   The majority.

Eurydice   From the minority?

Creon   In times like this the people prefer the familiar to the unknown.

Eurydice   Perhaps it's what they prefer, but what do they need?

Aleksy   The Prime Minster needs your support.

Eurydice   The Prime Minister needs broader advice / on

Aleksy   Pressing matters demand your attention, Prime Minister.

Creon   Quite. Yes. Is that . . . Tiresias?

Aleksy   I believe so.

Creon   What are they doing here?

Aleksy   You must go Prime Minister.

Creon   Of course.

Scene Four

The **Commissioner** *and* **Aleksy** *corner* **Ismene**.

Commissioner   This must be difficult for you.

Ismene   . . . It is.

Commissioner   Having one brother buried, and . . . unsure about the other. Did you hear from him?

Ismene   Pardon?

Commissioner   Polyneices. When last did you speak to him?

Ismene   The night he vanished, four years ago.

Commissioner   He hasn't contacted you since?

Ismene   No.

Commissioner   He never contacted you?

Ismene   What are you asking me?

Commissioner   It's a simple question. Did Polyneices make contact?

Aleksy   It's in your best interests to tell us what you know.

Beat.

Ismene   I know you had him. For eighteen months. I know you interrogated him and I know what that means.

Commissioner   Why do you think this?

Ismene   He emailed Ety.

Commissioner   When?

Ismene   Two hours before.

Aleksy   And you told no one?

Ismene   You didn't tell us you had him. Instead you told him his boys died, then let him go. Just like that. You could have stopped this. We could have.

Commissioner   We tailed him and he vanished.

Ismene   Does the Prime Minister know? I think he'll find it interesting.

Aleksy   He *did* find it interesting. Do you still have this email?

Beat.

Ismene   Uncle knew?

Aleksy   We had a general election to win. The party wanted to protect the Prime Minister's image, and we did not want the electorate to panic. Do you have this email?

Ismene   He knew? For months? You all did?

Commissioner   Do you have this email?

Ismene   Am I under arrest?

Aleksy   That email.

Ismene *takes out her phone, looks for the email.*

Aleksy   We'll take the phone.

Ismene   What? No!

The **Officers** *advance on her.*

Ismene   Okay, okay.

She hands it over, clearly shaken.

Commissioner   You are not under arrest. You may go.

Scene Five

Eteocles' *burial.*

The streets are packed with police and well-wishers. **Haemon,**
Antigone, Ismene, Kyria, Lyra, *the* **Commissioner, Aleksy,**
and **Nikomedes** *are among them.* **Nikomedes** *says the Janaza.*

Nikomedes   Allahum – maghfir lihayyinaa, wa mayyitinaa,
wa shaahidinaa, wa ghaa'ibinaa, wa sagheerinaa wa
kabeerinaa, wa thakarinaa wa 'unthaanaa.

Haemon *holds* **Antigone's** *hand until the coffin passes and the*
crowd begins to disperse.

Antigone *walks to* **Nikomedes**.

Antigone   Asalaam Alaikum.

Nikomedes   Wa alaykumu as-salam. My condolences.
Masha Allah. I haven't seen you in years.

Antigone   Your sermon for Eteocles and the Janaza, just
beautiful.

Nikomedes   I read the words from the Qur'an. Allah is to
be praised. What happened with Polyneices . . . Inna lillahi
wa inna ilayhi raji'oon.

Antigone   Ameen. No one else will say careful words for
him. I wanted to talk to you. I need another prayer.

Nikomedes   This is not the right time.

Antigone   Allah doesn't care about time.

Nikomedes (*laughs*)   First time we met, you also asked for
prayers. You were seven? Holding your father's hand tightly,
may he rest in peace, such defiance in your eyes. You refused
to pray with the women / and

Antigone   No, I refused to pray *behind* the men.

Nikomedes   You only let go of his hand after I promised to
make du'a just for you.

Antigone   I need another.

Nikomedes   Come to the mosque tomorrow? The new muezzin is so good. You know he is classically trained?

Antigone   Tomorrow is too late.

Nikomedes   What's the rush? Getting married or something?

Haemon *spots* **Antigone**.

Haemon   Antigone, I've been looking for you.

Antigone   I'll meet you at home.

Haemon   You sure?

Antigone   Yep, just catching up with . . .

Haemon   Beautiful Janaza by the way.

Nikomedes   Thank you.

Haemon *leaves*.

Antigone   I *am* getting married, I'd like you to lead my nikah, but I'm asking for Polyneices. We need Creon to release the body. You taught him and my dad. Will you talk to him?

Nikomedes   I want nothing to do with Polyneices. You know how many officers swarmed the mosque after he vanished? Young men they abducted for questioning? They asked me if I knew what Polyneices was planning, as if I would hide such a thing.

Antigone   Indefinitely detaining him / means they have him

Nikomedes   D'you know how many old men have been harassed? Sisters spat on?! They pull their hijabs! One was set on fire while she was wearing it, Antigone!

Antigone   I know it's not easy.

Nikomedes   Easy? This is my life! I'm under surveillance 24/7. When I'm preparing sermons, standing on the minbar, they are watching. I feel them in my head, among the verses. Young men are anxious, paranoid, the mental health repercussions . . . I'm not trained for any of this.

Antigone   I work with young men too, I know. I'm asking for his soul.

Nikomedes   No Imam will help you.

Antigone   What?

Nikomedes   The Prime Minister wants no grave site, no place for martyr-worship. If we help, if I'm seen to sympathise with a terrorist, I'd lose my licence. I could even go to prison.

Polyneices' *spirit appears on stage. Only* **Antigone** *can see him.*

Antigone   You can't accept this. Asking for his body is sympathy?

Nikomedes   Your brother went against fundamental principles of Islam.

Antigone   It's against fundamental principles of Islam not to bury him.

Nikomedes   The Prime Minster consulted us, the Muslim Council, to deter terrorism. The good of the many outweighs the needs of the few.

Antigone   You don't really believe that?!

Nikomedes   We had to agree. I'm sure Creon will bury him eventually.

Antigone   Are you all crazy?

Nikomedes   Do not be disrespectful.

Antigone   Unbelievable. You men.

Nikomedes   It is complicated, Antigone. You know it is.

Antigone   After one dies, burial must be immediate so the
soul can start its journey, otherwise an old unnatural
disturbance will . . . what's it? Plague the living? You taught
me this.

Nikomedes   I have never witnessed it.

Antigone   Course not. Who's done what he did, died, and
stayed among the living?

Polyneices' *spirit leaves the stage.*

Nikomedes   Do you want the public to hate you? Do you
want more attention?

Antigone   I run from attention!

Nikomedes   We have to keep the peace. Look at the
Mosque, look at what's happening,

Antigone   Look at the mosque! Look at what is happening!
The boys and girls have questions right? Can they talk to
you? Can you advise them? Schools kick them out for poor
performance, but don't check why they can't perform.
Ignore them when they speak, say they're suspicious when
they're quiet. Where do they fit? Polyneices used to follow
me everywhere. That baby, who slept in my arms how many
times?

Beat.

Nikomedes   He came to me with questions. It wasn't safe to
talk. He'd heard sermons online. Verses taken out of
context. Lies built on lies, that have nothing, nothing to do
with Islam! Grooming kids? It's so evil, Antigone. But still it's
no excuse. Many turn away. Because Polyneices didn't, the
police are everywhere.

Antigone   Are you angry with policing or Polyneices?
Them, we can change. He, is dead. Speak to Creon in the
name of Allah. Ask him to release Polyneices to us and we
will bury him quietly, peacefully, together.

Beat.

Nikomedes   I'm sorry. I cannot.

Chorus *of young Muslim boys.*

Chorus
   Remember those days of battle and brawn
   when the soul of the country was scattered and torn
   and the throne of power was empty and none
   of the candidates clamouring was clearly the one?

   And who won the race, who came number one,
   wasn't the loudest with the biggest drum,
   a towering presence familiar and strong
   but Creon Jafari, the underdog won.

   He's made life tougher, least for us all.
   See what happened to Ahmed Asmal.
   Four year old kid, silly and small
   drew his dad holding cucumbers up
   teacher asked: What's this you've drawn?
   Ahmed responds: coocumberbum.
   The teacher hears: cooker bomb
   calls the police who arrive with no qualms
   arrests this kid, takes him down town
   interrogating him, round and around
   the kid is shitting it, bricking it down:
   Where's my father? Where's my Mum?

   Then there's ten year old Asif Nahas
   who said he lived in a terrorist house
   he meant to say a two-storey house
   or meant to say a terraced house
   but the police raided his house
   grabbed his whole family, wearing them down.

   You make a mistake, tongue makes a slip,
   the government comes with guns on their hips.
   They call it Prevent, the programme is shit,
   designed to make teachers do surveillance, snitch
   on the kids that they're teaching, you hearing this shit?

And anyone who anyone thinks
seems suspicious is thrown on the list.
How the hell are we meant to feel British,
how are we meant to just be and just breathe
when they're pushing our families down to their knees?

Four thousand, five, that's the number it is
of us they've arrested, half of us kids.
And this database is never erased
though you're released you're still disgraced
and police always remember your face
they track you forever, there's never a place
where you're not paranoid, where you feel safe.

My sister now, always keeps schtum,
sits in her classroom sucking her thumb
to keep a low profile, acts like she's dumb
she's not the vibrant girl I knew and loved
she's now a ghost of the star that she was
feels like she doesn't fit in her class
feels like our country wants her to come last
in the race of life, she's letting them pass.

I miss those days of battle and brawn
when the soul of the country was scattered and torn
and the throne of power was empty and none
of the candidates clamouring was clearly the one.

Scene Six

Ismene's *flat.*

Antigone   Ismene! You in?

Ismene *is still shaken by* **Aleksy**'s *interrogation.*

Antigone   Ismene! Ismene! You okay?

Ismene   Antigone?

Antigone   Creon's never gonna let us have Nicey's body. Did you know that?

Ismene   W . . . What?

Antigone   Nikomedes told me.

Ismene   Indefinite detention just means until something changes. Something will change.

Antigone   Nikomedes said no Imam will bury him. So we will have to.

Ismene   And we will. We just have to be patient.

Antigone   You're not listening to me. The Muslim Council has banned . . . It's just us left, and you can't sit this one out again.

Ismene   Again?

Antigone   When they called us Pakis in school, Ety, Nicey and me always fought back. You just took it. Not now. We should go get his body, bathe him with warm water, camphor and leaves, wrap him in a white shroud and bury him facing Mecca.

Ismene   We can't do any of that. We have to wait. Things are very precarious right now.

Antigone   How is any of this legal.

Ismene   The State of Emergency. Uncle's law makes it so.

Antigone   And you helped him pass it?

Ismene   He is the first brown Prime Minister.

Antigone   Fuck that!

Ismene   We have to make this work. I have to, twice as good, twice as hard, remember?

Antigone   At what cost? Polyneices' soul?

Ismene   Breaking the law is haram.

Antigone   Not burying him is haram!

Ismene   Yes. We need a lawyer.

Antigone   That would take months. Fuck the law.

Ismene   To go against lawyers, magistrates, the Prime Minister? The entire machinery of this country?

Antigone   Creon should not rule over the dead.

Ismene   We have to be smart. We have to obey those in power.

Antigone   Men in power?

Ismene   If they are in power, yes.

Antigone   Not God?

Ismene   Allah put them there. Who understands the mind of God?

Antigone   They don't! There's no phallic pipeline to God's mind! God's not a dickhead.

Ismene (*laughs*)   You studied fiqh, learnt half the Qur'an, know the finest verses from the hadith, have written poetry yourself, but 'God's not a dickhead', incredible, seriously. Rumi should learn from you.

Antigone *laughs.*

Ismene   The public won't allow it. We will get his body. This is England.

Antigone (*laughs*)   On the way here, I heard men saying they wanna piss on him, women saying they wanna squat on his Muslim face. This is England. We have to get him out.

Ismene   Neenee, they interrogated me. It's not safe. Uncle knew what they did to Polyneices.

Beat.

Antigone   Then you know what he is capable of. I have to do this.

Ismene   You can't break into a secure facility.

Antigone   You're letting me down again. Last chance, Izzy.

Ismene   Nicey killed people! He let us down.

Antigone   He was confused! He told me he came to you, worried about Shari'ah law, persecuted Muslims, and you shut him down.

Ismene   I didn't know what to say.

Antigone   You just thought it was beneath you.

Ismene   He went to you first!

Antigone   I hadn't prayed in years, how could I / have

Ismene   You were his favourite! And you're better at theology than all of us. You could have cleared everything with one conversation, one cup of coffee, destroyed every argument / verse by verse

Antigone   I know. I know! Every morning I wake up and see his eyes. It's why I have to do something. It's on me.

Ismene   No. He killed people. He did that.

Antigone   We're still blood. Have to honour our dead.

Ismene   There'll be armed guards. It's impossible.

Antigone   I don't care.

Ismene   How are you not scared?

Antigone   'Cause it's the right thing to do!

Ismene   Antigone, wait! Wait! You are so irrational!

Antigone *exits.*

Ismene   So brave.

Later that night, a security guard comes home and speaks to her partner.

Chorus
> She came in the night, she gazed at the world,
> and the light of her eyes was a righteous sword,
> She saw the world for what it was,
> the darkness looming and me at its heart.
>
> We spoke of the dead, of life and of love,
> and her wish to give back what came from above,
> and the teeth of the city cutting her off.
>
> She called me a canine, the city's sharp point,
> bleeding its citizens of their right to show love,
> a dog of the urban, a blight in her world,
> and I couldn't respond, and I couldn't respond.
>
> She spoke of old ways, still practised back home,
> twenty-four hours and the deed would be done,
> and the Gods above would carry souls on,
> like my mother's, father's, ancestors', long gone.
>
> Who're we to break that line? Who am I to be unkind?
> I lay down my sword and gave her the key.
> She gathered her wings and entered the darkness
> and knelt by her love, and set her love free.

Scene Seven

Antigone *and* **Haemon**'s *flat.*

Antigone *enters and runs into the bathroom.* **Haemon** *speaks to her through the door.*

Haemon   Antigone? I've been so worried. Lyra didn't know where you were. You didn't come home last night. Did you see my calls?

Antigone   Battery died.

Haemon   You okay? Hungry? Can you open the door?

Antigone   Can you give me a few?

Haemon   Of course. Eteocles was a good man. He didn't deserve . . . His funeral was something. The procession, the whole city, love pouring out like that.

Antigone   I have two brothers.

Haemon   Yes but . . . When is his funeral?

Antigone *laughs.*

Haemon   Are you laughing?

Beat.

Have you spoken to Ismene? She won't answer my calls.

Antigone   Do you agree with Creon's terror laws? Stripping Nicey's citizenship?

Haemon   The country voted for it.

Antigone   You know what he wants to do?

Haemon   What does he want to do? Did something happen?

Beat.

Let's just go somewhere? Get out of the city, somewhere calm.

Antigone   His body was starting to rot. I couldn't leave him like that.

Antigone *steps out of the bathroom still carrying a bag.*

Antigone   I have to finish it.

Haemon   Finish what?

Antigone   Creon wants to leave Nicey unburied. I said the Janaza. Washed his body. Guards came, so I got interrupted. I have to wrap him up. I was gonna ask you for help.

Haemon   Help?

Antigone   I can't turn him over on my own. He is heavy.

Beat.

Haemon   My God. Don't expect . . . Is this against the law?

Antigone   So you *do* agree with your father. Good to know who you're loyal to.

Haemon   You! You're my wife, but what have you done?

Antigone   Wife to be. I wanted to free his soul.

Haemon   When did you start believing in that?

Antigone   My brother has a soul.

Haemon   Yes. Of course. I mean you stepped away from . . . you haven't practiced in a while, and this is a big thing to do, to bury a terrorist who / is not

Antigone   I'M BURYING MY BROTHER! That's all I'm doing. His face was . . . lips torn, his chest . . . bullets . . . they just dumped him there.

Haemon   Oh, Antigone.

Antigone   Don't touch me. Creon is using that law to make a political point. Keeping my brother above ground . . . it's the worst thing you can do to a Muslim.

Haemon   He wouldn't do that. This is England.

Antigone *laughs.*

Haemon   That's preposterous.

Antigone   He assigned his own private security to the body. Not the police. Why?

Beat.

You're thinking now.

Haemon   This is not public yet. I can try to talk to him.

Antigone   He won't change his mind.

Haemon   You don't know that.

Antigone   I have to finish what I started.

Antigone *moves to exit.*

Haemon   Antigone, wait. Wait.

Antigone   There's no time. Come or . . . you can leave me.

Haemon   Leave you?

Antigone   I'm making it simple for you.

Haemon   Look, Neenee . . . your hair. Polyneices made a choice and died because of it.

Antigone   His kids. He wasn't thinking clearly.

Haemon   That does not excuse what he did.

Antigone   Doesn't mean we can desecrate his body.

Haemon   I never really knew him. It's hard to empathise with someone who caused you so much pain. Don't let him affect us, our plans . . . the youth centres, one stop shops for young misfits, remember that? We have our whole lives ahead.

Antigone   I won't be able to live my life if I don't do this.

Haemon's *phone rings.*

Haemon   It's your sister.

Antigone   Don't answer it.

Haemon   Hold on a sec. Hello? Yes, she is here.

Antigone   Put it down, Haemon / put it

Haemon   She won't listen to me / she won't do anything

Antigone   I'm going.

Haemon   Hold on, Izzy. Antigone, just wait.

Antigone *opens the door to find* **Eurydice**.

Haemon   Mum?
Izzy, I have to go.

He hangs up.

Eurydice   Won't you invite me in?

Haemon   Sorry.

She enters.

Eurydice   Antigone?

Antigone   Sorry.

Antigone *leaves.*

Eurydice   How is she?

Haemon   I . . . I don't know.

Eurydice   How are wedding plans?

Haemon   Is this really why you're here?

Eurydice   No.

Haemon   Don't you have one of your superwomen council meetings?

Eurydice   We had a conference call earlier. I needed their advice.

Haemon   About what?

Eurydice   Well . . . it's not too late.

Haemon   For what?

Eurydice   What her brother did . . . if you marry her, you have to carry it. You don't have to. You can do anything you want.

Haemon   She didn't do it. He did.

Eurydice   I know, but you are the Prime Minister's son.

Haemon   He is your husband.

Eurydice   And this, all this, compromises him.

Haemon   You know what he plans to do? To leave the body unburied forever?

Beat.

Eurydice   Are you sure?

Haemon   You didn't know?

Eurydice   I would have tried to stop him.

Haemon   Mother?

Eurydice   I swear. Not that I'd have been successful. Creon shared everything with me . . . hospital visits, race-hate mail, how he practiced a firm handshake for hours; he always took my advice, but the change is drastic, the election ate him and spat out this . . . I don't know who this is.

Haemon   Mother . . .

Eurydice   I have to be supportive. I do not want to create conflict in his office.

Haemon   Do you still love him?

Eurydice   He is still there, somewhere. I need a few hours away from all that. I can't go home. The press are everywhere. Can I stay. Just for a while?

Haemon   Of course, Mum.

Outside Downing Street.

Officer *enters.*

A **Chorus** *of photographers and journalists.*

Chorus
    Did you see that officer
    running to Downing Street?
    Did you catch his words,
    was he vexed? Was he pissed?

Where there any signs of stress?
What's the story? What's the best
way to frame his entrance?
What could be the headline?

What concerns the nation?
What are they afraid to say?
For the story I could write,
how much will they pay?

Should I give them what they want?
Or give them what they need?
Who benefits from this story?
Who starves and who feeds?

Should we whip them to a frenzy
or let them go to sleep?
Should I follow that officer,
discover his secret?

Should I think of repercussions,
deeply consider it?
Should I write them down,
then meticulously bin it?

Should I let what might happen
stop me from my path?
Or should I acknowledge the chaos
and decide that it'll pass?

Should I capture his picture,
like a snapshot scripture,
share on the socials
and let them do the maths?

Should I set the stage for rage?
Hope it turns to wrath?

Where's the moral compass?
Where does its needle point?
Does our hunger for stories
make our needle blunt?

What if there was silence
and we published . . . air?
What might fill the quiet?
What is there that's rare?

Why did that officer
charge in so quickly?
Check you have batteries!
Get your camera ready!

Scene Eight

Downing Street.

Creon *is surrounded by the* **Commissioner**, *officials and civil servants.*

Commissioner   I wanted to commend you on a progressive show of strength.

Creon   Thank you.

Commissioner   I also want to expand my support in matters regarding the attack. I have men at my disposal to set up checkpoints around the facility?

Creon   Facility?

Commissioner   The detention centre. Where the terrorist is held.

Creon   Have I requested assistance?

Commissioner   No, I was . . . pre-empting your request.

Creon   I have reassigned some of your men from my private security detail. They now report directly to me. The matter is in hand.

Commissioner   Prime Minister, this is . . . highly unusual.

Creon   Yet it is the circumstance in which we find ourselves.

Commissioner   How else can we help?

Creon   Police the streets, enforce the law. Do not break it and deal swiftly with anyone who does.

Commissioner   Only an imbecile would risk treason and imprisonment.

Creon   And imbeciles walk among us . . . all I trust now is data analysis, algorithmic precision, targeted advertising to our electorate. That is what delivered the election, and it will guide me going forward.

Eurydice *and* **Aleksy** *enter with an* **Officer**.

Creon   Ah, here he comes, the hilt to my sword. Aleksy.

Aleksy   Sir, this officer from your detail requests to speak with you. He says it is urgent.

Creon   Ah, what can I do for you?

Officer   Prime Minister, Commissioner.

Commissioner   At ease.

Beat.

Officer   Big fan. I think you're doing a great job.

Creon   Well, what it is?

Officer   Big thing, sir. Don't wanna say. Don't know how.

Commissioner   Are you stupid?

Officer   Bit harsh. I'm just / trying to do my job.

Creon   Speak or get out!

Officer   The body. Someone's gone and tampered with it.

Eurydice   What do you mean tampered with it?

Officer   In detention. Right there. They washed the body with stuff. Closed the eyes, combed the hair, cleaned the wounds, as if they wanted his soul to rest, done a really lovely job like some weird muslamic voodoo thing.

Creon   Who did this?

Officer   No idea. Never seen 'em before in my life.

Creon   Well, where are they?

Officer   Oh, in the van.

Commissioner   Well, go and get him!

Officer   Alright, keep your hair on.

The **Officer** *salutes and leaves.*

Creon   This reflects badly on you, Commissioner.

Commissioner   Me?

Creon   These are your men. Do you have anything to say?

Commissioner   Perhaps it's er . . . the secret service? To destabilise your leadership?

Aleksy   The secret service? Who knew of Polyneices, where he lived, his views, yet couldn't track him leaving to Syria?

Creon   It wasn't them.

Aleksy   In the early days of your campaign, there were those in the party who could not stand the idea of a man like you claiming the highest office. They loved the caretaker, but ruling the house?

Creon   These men are still trying to undermine me.

Aleksy   They want it suggested you are not a man of your word, that because Polyneices was a relative, you allowed this. A smear campaign. They bribed your officers to let this happen.

Commissioner   Never!

The **Officer** *returns with* **Antigone** *in handcuffs.*

Eurydice   This is Antigone.

Officer   And? Look at her bag. She's the one who did it.

Creon   Antigone. Look at me. Is this true?

Antigone   Hundred per cent.

Officer   Told you.

Creon   Leave.

Officer   So . . . is there some sorta reward for /
apprehending a terror sympathiser?

Creon   GET OUT!

Officer *exits.*

Creon   Antigone.

Antigone   Creon.

Aleksy   Prime Minster, be careful.

Creon   How are you? We haven't spoken or seen each other
in a while.

Antigone   I wish it had remained that way.

Creon   . . .What do you have against me?

Antigone   Are you serious? You threw Polyneices out.

Creon   He left of his own accord. And you followed.

Antigone   That's what you tell yourself?

Eurydice   You didn't know about the law?

Antigone   Everyone knew.

Creon   So, you broke the law?

Antigone   I laid my brother to rest.

Creon   You broke the law?

Antigone   I didn't have any extremist material. I terrorised
no one, I didn't kill anybody.

Creon   You broke the law.

Antigone   The law is a shit show, to make Britons stateless.

Creon   To make the countries in which they were radicalised responsible.

Antigone   He was *misguided* here, so we are responsible. You lied to parliament.

Creon   They were aware of my intentions.

Antigone   To rule over dead bodies?

Creon   To protect our way of life.

Antigone   Individual liberty, respect, tolerance, is our way of life, right?

Creon   The rule of law is our way of life.

Antigone   Some laws are beyond men. Some rights are inalienable, they belong to Earth, they are older than this country, than the concept of countries. To leave his body like that? Faith says he should be buried. I washed him, said the Janaza, the journey of his soul begins.

Creon   You're an idiot.

Antigone   You're an arrogant prick.

Eurydice   Antigone, calm down.

Creon   Eurydice, keep out of this, it's not your business.

Eurydice   She is family, it *is* my business.

Creon   Why would you do this?

Aleksy   She is completely unrepentant.

Eurydice   You could plead temporary insanity?

Antigone   He's the crazy one.

Creon   Dead or alive, she helped Polyneices, she aided a terrorist, she broke the law, so I have to ensure punishment. What sort of example would I set if I didn't?

Eurydice   We need a change of perspective / because thinking

Creon   Find her sister. Bring her here.

Aleksy   She's been walking the corridors, guilt pouring out of her.

An **Officer** *leaves.*

Antigone   Ismene didn't do anything. This is between us.

Creon   Both of you will be charged.

Antigone   The best of you is he who is best to his family. The Prophet Muhammad – peace be upon him – said that.

Creon   You weed-smoking infidel, quoting the prophet?

Antigone   I've confessed. I'll go to jail.

Creon   You don't have a choice.

Antigone   So leave Ismene out of this. I buried him alone.

Creon   Aren't you conflicted at all? All this for an actual terrorist?

Antigone   For my brother, like we are supposed to, like faith asks us. Hate the sin, not the sinner.

Creon   Eteocles was your brother too. You are insulting his memory, dishonouring him.

Antigone   Burying both is honourable.

Creon   He attacked us!

Antigone   Every prayer starts Bismillah ar-rahman ar-raheem.

Creon   Stop.

Antigone   In the name of God, the Compassionate, the Merciful. We are supposed to be compassionate and merciful, because when we die we can only carry our good deeds to heaven, to Akhirah. What are yours?

Creon   You, lecturing me on Islam?

Antigone   My faith is mine, yours is yours, but compassion, mercy are / the

Creon   Those compassionate merciful teachings drove Polyneices.

Antigone   You know they didn't.

Creon   They did.

Antigone   The same teachings drove Eteocles.

Creon   Islam's burial laws clash with our laws.

Antigone   They clash with your law. You're not the country.

Creon   I speak for the country.

Antigone   You speak for yourself.

Creon   When you die, go to hell, show mercy there, but here you will be found guilty of treason and you will be charged.

Ismene *is dragged in by an* **Officer**.

Creon   You! I gave you a job in my office! Aleksy wanted you removed but I refused. I expected to be stabbed in the back, this is politics, but not by you. Admit it, you buried him too.

Ismene   I did.

Antigone   She didn't!

Ismene   My brother had to be buried.

Antigone   Who buried him? Whose hands?

Ismene   We will go to jail together.

Antigone   No we won't.

Ismene   I'm your big sister. It's my job to protect you.

Antigone   She couldn't commit a crime if she tried.

Ismene   I'm her accomplice.

Antigone   Why d'you want to go to jail? You are free of me now.

Ismene   I don't want to be free of you. I've missed you, so much, your chaos.

Antigone *laughs.*

Ismene   You're laughing?

Antigone   I won't cry in front of him.

Creon   You hearing this Aleksy?

Ismene   Allah does not burden a soul with more than it can bear. I can do this, let me help.

Antigone   Be the one who survives . . . right? Live in Allah's light.

Ismene   All these years, you've been running from Islam. Why now?

Antigone   I wasn't running from Islam! I was running from everything around it! So overbearing! I couldn't tell what was Muslim culture, Arabic tradition or God! The pressure to do what you wanted, the boys, men, society, this country, all clashing with what I wanted to do! I tried to smoke it all away, then Nicey died, Creon passed that law and the madness cleared. I needed to bury my brother, faith teaches I should. Simple. For the first time in my whole life, in my soul, no conflict. Such clarity, Izzy, I wish you could feel this.

Ismene   Admit I buried him with you.

Eurydice   I think it's clear what this is.

Creon   One's lost her mind, the other wants to.

Aleksy   Prison will sort them out.

Eurydice   You'll destroy your son's fiancée?

Aleksy There are other fields for him to plough, sandpits to piss in.

Eurydice Don't do this.

Creon I'm not, the law is.

Commissioner So it is settled. The charge is treason?

Creon Yes.

Aleksy No bail or visits, in the interest of public safety and security.

Antigone I buried my brother, I was right to break your law, nothing will change that.

Creon You are a danger to this great nation, you are a threat to civilised peoples everywhere, you will face justice, and I will see it done. Take them away.

Officers *take* **Antigone** *and* **Ismene** *away.*

End of Act One.

Act Two

Scene One

Police station: **Officers** *drag* **Antigone** *and* **Ismene** *in.*

Ismene   Oi get off! You're hurting her! Let go of my arm! If I bleed, I'll sue you. You know all this is bullshit? You know this isn't right?

Officers *throw them in separate cells. The bars clang shut and they leave.*

Ismene   Antigone? Did he hurt you? You okay? Say something!

Antigone
This is my freckled forehead
These are its deep lines
This is the furrowed crease of my brows
These are my tired eyes
These are its dark waters
These are its grey bags and weighted worries
This is my narrow neck and its heavy duty
This is my throat
This is its forming song
These are my quiet shoulders and simple arms
This is its trembling work

Those are the courts of the city
Those are its laws glinting
Those are its chambers combusting
Those judges grease its work
Those leaders fuel its fire
Those officers churn its pistons
Those journalists belch its voice
Those activists spin its raging wheels
This is its fixed course

I saw my brother's chest
I saw his flat heart

I saw his petal-thin eyelids
I scented his soul with oil
I held the white cloth like a fallen flag
I placed it over his body
I prayed his name
And now, I will sleep.

Ismene   Oh Nene.

Scene Two

Chorus: **Lyra**, **Youth Group**, **Tiresias** *and* **Citizens**.

Lyra   I need Antigone. Can't do this without her. Can't watch the news, the things they say about her: that she's a car crash, a mix of weed and arrogance, an entitled bitch. They don't know shit.

Public Chorus   They arrested her for tampering with the bones of a murderer, a terrorist.

She's kinda brave through.

There's gonna be a trial, and if found guilty, maximum sentence.

Lyra   It's mad. It's shitty.

Public Chorus   She tampered with his body?

Tampered with his body?

Tampered with his body?

What does that mean?

My uncle works in parliament and word on the street is she washed the body, wrapped it in a sheet.

That's what this is? Because she cleaned him?

Terror law says she can't do nothing.

He's no longer British, countries won't touch him. Mosques can't touch him, it's against the law.

He was lying there, dust on the floor.

That's why she washed him?

That's just bad luck.

Tiresias   Her family is cursed. There's bad blood pouring from the them. It's gonna get worse. Death is ruled by an ancient force, and this will unleash Old Testament God, truly bad karma, us mortals can't stop.

Public Chorus   The kind that don't sleep. Sort that don't slumber.

Stop! You're scaring me.

Everything that's happening, I think it's Creon.

It's all him.

That, we agree on.

He is human, just have to change his mind.

Changing Creon's mind? Utterly pointless, like using strings to hold back a tide.

Let's consider this deeply, I know its entwined in terrorism and murder, reprehensible crime that might've claimed your friend, might have claimed mine, but he killed his own brother.

Consider his mind?

Some sort of insanity?

Your words not mine.

Fine, who can prove it?

Doesn't matter, he's dead.

We can ponder on it but it's above our heads. I don't think 'terrorist' frightened in bed, 'cause I know they got him. It's over, he is dead.

And she probably thinks this too.

Like it's not about terror.

It's not about law.

That's my brother's head.

It should be covered up.

Keep rats from nibbling on his crotch.

Oi!

Just saying, what she did was brave.

Burying your brother . . .

You'd do that for me right? If someone tried to stop you?

I'd take away their life!

Exactly! So, someone should stop this.

But it's Creon, man's a dark tide.

Lyra   Let's do something then.
Let's change the tide.

Lyra *takes out her phone, bends over it typing urgently. The youth group gather round, also typing urgently.*

Scene Three

Downing Street.

Aleksy *in his office. A loud commotion outside.* **Haemon** *pushes in restrained by police.*

Haemon   Where is he? Where is my father? Get your hands off me.

Aleksy   Leave him, let him go. He will calm down.

Officer *releases him.*

You have come about Antigone? It is not a good time. The Prime Minister is / tied up in

Haemon   Where is he?!

Aleksy *dials a number.*

Aleksy   Your son is here. It is about her. He is . . . composed.

Aleksy *puts down the phone.*

He will be out momentarily.

Haemon *paces.* **Creon** *enters followed by the* **Commissioner**, **Eurydice** *and other* **Aides**.

Creon   So Haemon, no doubt, you've heard the charges. Are you furious or do you accept what's been done?

Haemon   I'm your son. You have always given me sound advice, provided great opportunities. Nothing means more than being aligned with you.

Creon   This is how it should be. What more could a father want?

Your mother is level-headed, amicable. It's why we've stood together for so long. Never lose your head over personal relationships. The law is steadfast. Emotions are not. Soon as the fires between thighs wane, relationships falter. Nothing is worse. This is your way out. Distance yourself. Let Antigone marry her brother in hell. Sympathising with a terrorist, honouring a murderer? My own niece? She thought it would put me at a crossroads, but the road ahead is clear. Aleksy advised me well, the data proved this is what the people want. She can cry compassion, mercy, but if I let her free, the country would not follow where I lead. We should defend those who live by the law, discipline those who don't.

Haemon Dad, all that separates us from other animals is reason. God, Allah, Yahweh or the sheer luck of evolution gave us that. Without reason, choosing when or not to follow, we become sheep, meat machines. Because you raised me to reason, I hope you take this well. I believe you've reasoned badly.

My job centres the people. I'm a publicist, I have to know how to talk and listen to them. I am brilliant at it. On buses, trains, taxis, phones, online, they are talking about her, their words flying around us right now, in the very air between our teeth.

They say 'She's suffered enough, she don't deserve this', 'She didn't want her brother to become rat food'. 'I hope my friends do that for me!' They message each other, write poetry. The most searched term online is Muslim funeral. The Janaza is trending, musicians have remixed it. Kids act this out in playgrounds, wanting to be her, wrapping their siblings in sheets, graffiti artists, tagging her name everywhere. This is the country. This is their pulse. They want compassion, mercy, reason. Don't be rigid with the law.

What was it you taught me about sailing? Haul your sheets too taught and the boat goes over, but a little slack and you sail smooth. I want you to be a great leader, your victories are my victories, I campaigned for you, so please listen.

The gathered murmur in agreement.

Eurydice Really good points from the both of you. I think you should consider each other's words carefully.

Creon Is that so? Anyone else think I should listen to this boy?

Eurydice If he is right, should his age matter?

Creon You think you can lecture your own father?

Haemon Islam teaches if your parents are wrong, you can tell them, even if your father is Prime Minister. You just have to be respectful.

Creon   What are you talking about?! Which Islam? Which hadith? Which sunnah? Which school of thought?

Haemon   You tell me. You were raised by the mosque, you were a scholar.

Creon   You told him about me, Eurydice?

Haemon   Antigone did. You and her dad studied together.

Creon   And for that, you think I should pardon her treason?

Eurydice   The archbishop says what you are doing is un-Christian Creon. Previous home secretaries think this is wrong.

Creon   They are out of touch.

Eurydice   And you believe you are?

Aleksy   The majority still support the Prime Minister, the data is there.

Haemon   What data?! The country disagrees with you.

Aleksy   Your woke millennials on Twitter?

Creon   They should tell me what to think?

Haemon   They should inform your thinking in a true democracy.

Aleksy   He was elected to think for them.

Haemon   No one man should have all that power.

Aleksy   The law is the law, and she broke it.

Haemon   He broke it first! Human rights, already enshrined in law and in God's law. Allah specifically / said

Creon   You've never entered a mosque! What do you know of Allah? You are using concepts you don't understand to critique this Great Britain. Allah said if your wife is disobedient, you can beat her.

Haemon   A mistranslation of 'daraba'. It can mean 'beating' or 'leaving', depends on what you choose to believe.

Creon   It says what it says.

Haemon   You don't read the Qur'an, the Qur'an reads you. Heard that before?

Creon   If its language can be so easily weaponised, then the Qur'an is dangerous.

Haemon   More so than the Bible? How many countries violently colonised by Christians? There are right wing Hindus lynching Muslims in India! Buddhist monks assaulting women! Anything can be a weapon in the wrong hands, even the law! What you sacrificed, I understand, but this is wrong. You know better. Following Islam, with utmost sincerity is incredible, but being rigid can lead to horrendous acts, dark consequences.

Creon   This is what Polyneices did.

Eurydice   Punishing a brilliant young woman?

Haemon   Destroying my life?

Eurydice   These are dark consequences too.

Creon   You compare me to Polyneices?

Eurydice   Your actions, not you.

Aleksy   Prime Minister, this is beneath you.

Haemon   Think! What's fair? Antigone is just like you, rejected rigidity to find herself. Forget you are a politician, use your heart. Antigone makes this personal, so use your person. Get out in front, talk about the shades of Islam. Be expansive, nuanced, deep, meaningful.

Aleksy   Are you mad?

Haemon   A press conference. I can set this up.

Creon   I should discuss, on television, Islamic philosophy? To dissect the pros and cons of what, Shari'ah law?

Haemon   Yes!

Eurydice   The party does have a history of Islamophobia. You can use this to address that.

Creon   You want me to do that? To compare Shari'ah to British law? A man of my heritage, Eurydice? Have you forgotten what I've been through?

Aleksy   Very poor advice.

Creon   If I criticise Islam, the Muslim community and liberal voters will destroy me. If I sympathise, conservative voters will. If I do nothing, the right wing press will label me a militant in Westminster.

Haemon   You can talk of belief whilst not believing, you can separate religion from the man.

Creon   Which country do you live in? Where do you think you are? Beyond this city, these cosmopolitan elites, this festering pit of privilege and wealth, the silent majority, most of whom still worship Churchill, won't understand or care why I'd want to discuss concepts they fear. We all look the same to them, I'll burn every bridge I have built. I won't do it.

Eurydice   This is bigger than you.

Haemon   Bigger than being Asian.

Creon   What do you understand about it, you selfish / little

Eurydice   Creon!

Aleksy   This has gone far enough.

Haemon   What do you have to lose?

Creon   Everything!

Eurydice   You'll lose everything if you carry on this way.

Creon   Everything he says is for her.

Haemon   For you, me, the country / the future

Aleksy   We need to move on, Prime Minister.

Creon   Let me make this clear. Even if the prophet himself and angel Jibreel come. Even if they speak in orthodox Arabic and their words turn to calligraphy in the air, the prophet's like blooming petals and the angel's like golden flames. Even if the flames and flowers swirl into the purest pleas for her and Polyneices, nothing will change my mind. You'll never marry her. She will die before you do.

Eurydice   Who are you?

Haemon   That will cause another death.

Eurydice   Haemon / I think we should go home and

Creon   You threatening me, boy?

Haemon   I make promises not threats.

Aleksy   Officers, arrest him!

Eurydice   He hasn't committed a crime!

Aleksy   Now!

The **Officers** *move towards* **Haemon**, **Eurydice** *blocks their path.*

Haemon   You will regret this.

Haemon *runs out, bumps into* **Nikomedes** *who pulls him away.*

Eurydice   What are you doing?

Aleksy   He might be dangerous.

Eurydice   Creon, I will not be ignored.

Creon   He won't save those women.

Commissioner   We can't charge Ismene. We know she wasn't there. We have to release her soon.

Creon   Fine. But for Antigone, make it known the Prime Minister wishes her taken to the most godforsaken prison. Ensure she has to fight for food and water, and after each fight, solitary confinement. I want her in court tomorrow. Let her pray to whoever she wants. She will learn, the law is the law, it governs everyone, without exception. Get out!

Aleksy, *the* **Commissioner** *and* **Aides** *leave,* **Creon** *moves to follow them.*

Eurydice   Creon.

Creon *turns around.*

Eurydice   We planned to retire together by the sea, from there work quietly to leave the world in a better state than when we entered it. Our lives, values, sacred beliefs, our souls were aligned. But you are so far from me. I . . . I want to be supportive, but these laws . . . you've become pugilistic, arrogant, disrespectful of me in public, tried to have your own son arrested! What's gotten into you?

Creon   Step son.

Creon *walks away.*

Eurydice   Creon, Creon!

Eurydice *makes a call.*

Gather all the women who donated, barristers, tech, Fortune 500, venture capital, oil and industry . . . I'm calling an emergency meeting. Three hours. Creon's out of control.

Scene Four

Outside the mosque.

Nikomedes *gives* **Haemon** *some water. A young scholar keeps watch.*

Nikomedes   Breathe. I don't think we were followed.

Haemon   What were you doing there, Nikomedes?

Nikomedes   I wanted to talk to someone, maybe Creon.

Haemon   You could have been arrested. They're lunatics. Creon is the craziest.

Nikomedes   Do not speak ill of you father.

Haemon   Step father. STEP father.

Nikomedes   Have you seen Antigone?

Haemon   No visitors allowed. I heard her though, reciting the call to prayer.

Nikomedes   Allah uakbar! Antigone is suffering for my mistakes. I chaired the Muslim Council. I approved Creon's law.

Haemon   No one knew his true intentions.

Nikomedes   You know parents of the victims wear t-shirts saying '#BuryHate #ChooseLove'. Posting them online. Their parents, Haemon, it stunned me. If they could forgive!

Haemon   Creon ignores all of them.

Nikomedes   How can he?

Haemon   I just want her home. I don't care about any of this. I want my wife. You understand? She is everything.

Nikomedes   Creon can't ignore all those people.

Haemon   Only ultra rich lobbyists, private investors bankrolling his government can change Creon's mind, but they won't.

Nikomedes   Why?

Haemon   They like the country as it is, small governments, less regulated worlds in which they can exploit people. Antigone represents everything they hate.

Nikomedes   They are human like we are. If I could speak with them I think / I could

Haemon   They'll look at your thobe and dismiss you. Look, Antigone is still trending, yet all this is just numbers, clicks, profit to them. They track and forget.

Beat.

Nikomedes   All that is digital, we need to make it real. How many news outlets can you contact?

Haemon   All of them. Why?

Nikomedes   Invite them to the court house. Let's make something unforgettable . . . a real old fashioned debate: We'll make those investors see Creon is a waste of their money, he's gone too far, because of him they'll lose the party and the country. Antigone can do this, we have to make her take control of the narrative. It's a girl burying a boy.

Haemon   A sister burying her brother.

Nikomedes   The world sees it that way.

Haemon   And it's them against the world.

Beat.

Haemon   It might work . . . Okay . . . right.

Haemon *and* **Nikomedes** *huddle together.*

Scene Five

Outside **Ismene***'s flat.*

A **Police Officer** *leads* **Ismene** *out and removes her handcuffs. Another* **Officer** *drops a cardboard box beside her.*

Officer   The Prime Minister no longer requires your service. Sorry, love.

Ismene   Of course you are.

The **Officer** *leaves.* **Eurydice** *enters.*

Eurydice   Ismene.

Ismene   I no longer work for him. I can't help you.

Eurydice   We used to live under the same roof, don't treat me like a stranger. What you tried to do for your sister. Very brave.

Ismene   I don't think you should be seen with me.

Eurydice   Antigone is / causing problems.

Ismene   Antigone is showing the world the coward Creon Jafari truly is. Sorry.

Eurydice   No need to apologise.

Ismene   To hide behind a dead body? If he stepped forward, talked about British activities in the Middle East, those wars, refugees, 50 per cent of British Muslims live in poverty, budget cuts to services, all those lost, lost boys, if he told that story, owned it, it would be inspiring! Instead he does this, it's despicable.

Eurydice   You've always been so quiet.

Ismene   Britain has buried this narrative for too long. It makes men like Creon *and* Polyneices.

Eurydice   Creon wasn't always like this.

Ismene   He is my uncle. I know exactly who he is. How can you still stand by him?

Eurydice   I'm a woman. I know what it is to want power in a country ruled by men, by white men. Creon used to say things in meetings they'd ignore, then repeat moments later, to applause. I shared his struggle, believed as Prime Minster he'd take care of everyone. But my caretaker has become a tyrant and I have to do something about it. I was hoping you would join me.

Ismene   Me?

Eurydice   A few women would like to meet you. We want to act. We are taking steps to move against Creon.

Ismene   I don't trust you.

Eurydice   You sister loves my son. He loves her. Since they met Haemon has become more focused and driven than he's ever been. The way he challenged Creon, he stands taller, cares so much, about so much, wanting to start a charity? A network of youth centres? He's become all I hoped he'd be. I will not have that taken away from me, so I can't have Antigone taken away from him. I need you. You want to save your sister? We can help.

Beat.

Ismene   Only women?

Eurydice   Thirty to forty, powerful ones, heads of industries, wealthy, overlooked, angry and motivated.

Ismene   You need real numbers, women's groups, activist networks, grass roots organisers, and they won't care about your money.

Eurydice   We know. They won't talk to us. They don't trust us. But they'll talk to you.

Beat.

Ismene   Let's go.

Scene Six

Chorus*: members of the public talk, glued to their screens.*

Public Chorus
    Do you follow Haemon? I think he's lost it.
    Every single photo he posts is of her.

He's gone from PR and profit
football and horses
to quotes from the prophet
and photos of the girl.

He just loves her!

Love's the last thing that humbles man
in this world
Sailors come back for it
shepherds go out for it

Didn't gods start huge wars for it?

There's no love between this father and son.

Now, it's pure simmering rage.

Antigone is their war, the country is their stage.

I can't watch this. Too much suffering. It will break my
heart for good.

They are taking Antigone to be charged!

Creon can't do this. No one should.

Outside the courthouse: **Antigone**, *handcuffed, flanked by*
Officers *walks through a mob of people. Some wear #choselove*
#buryhate t-shirts, with flags and banners. **Lyra**, **Athan** *and*
Strom *are among them. A cross-section of the British public is*
represented. Cameras flash.

Haemon *and* **Nikomedes** *(in disguise), and* **Tiresias** *are among*
them. A call and response rises among them all.

Chorus
Choose Love! Bury Hate!
Lock her up and throw the key!
Choose Love! Bury Hate!
Lock her up and throw the key!
Choose Love! Bury Hate!
Lock her up and throw the key!

Choose Love! Bury Hate!
Antigone! We love you!

Antigone   Why are you all here?

Chorus
You did nothing wrong, love!
We know it's not fair.
You were just being kind.
They wanna destroy you.

Antigone   They won't, don't worry.

Chorus/Men (*laughs*)   Yeah! Prison will.

Chorus/Women   That's not funny.

Antigone   It's okay. Britain's got a hostile environment for empathy, specially from men. I know boys confused like that.

Chorus   I think you're confused love.

Antigone   Yeah, whatever.

Haemon (*whispering*)   I can't do this.

Nikomedes (*whispering*)   You have to, it's her only chance.

Cameras start rolling. People surround her with microphones.

Haemon   You did this to yourself, should have followed the law.

Antigone   It was harsh and unnecessary.

Haemon   Your religion is harsh and unnecessary.

Antigone   Who said that?

Chorus   Why does it make people terrorists? And diminish women?

Antigone   Piss off, not answering that. You know how inane, ignorant you sound?

Chorus   See! She can't defend it.

Antigone   Why do we always do this? Every time something happens, we have this same discussion, ask the same stupid questions?

Haemon   What should we ask?

Antigone   Okay, how about . . . when did this really really start? Iraq, Afghanistan, Bosnia, Somalia, Suez, the crusades? Why did Britain start painting Muslims as barbaric? How many invasions did that legitimize? When you traumatize whole nations, whole worlds, what happens to the children? Those are the questions you should ask.

Haemon   But Muslim men treat women like property, makes them meek, forces them to wear hijabs?

Antigone   Are you dumb? Am I meek?

Nikomedes *laughs.*

Antigone   Why'd you ask? Is it to paint Muslim men as oppressors? Why are you so obsessed with what we wear? It's none of your business. It's never asked why Muslim women are attacked *for* wearing hijabs. But this is England, hijab or not, Muslim or not, aren't women attacked? Even by police? How many are killed by partners each week?

Chorus   What are you on about?

Antigone   The world has a problem, it isn't Islam, it's men and power. How they feel without it, what they do to get it, what that makes them do. My brother had none, couldn't even talk in his mosque, look what happened. But faith teaches compassion, even for murderers.

Chorus
Never! No!
That's that Shari'ah law talking.
Want that taking over British law?

Antigone   Shari'ah means path, that animals take to watering holes in the desert. It's a travel guide, that's it, like asking Londoners for directions. Everyone knows, nobody knows: this way, that way, Google it, good luck!

Chorus *laughs.*

Antigone   There are so many versions, it's a mess. And I like mess, ask my fiancé.

Chorus   You can't follow Shari'ah and British law anyway.

Antigone   Yes you can. Eteocles upheld both and died protecting us. Like me, he was born here, British to the bone.

Chorus   Polyneices killed people. You excusing that?

Antigone   No!

Polyneices' *spirit appears on stage. Only* **Antigone** *can see him.* **Antigone** *speaks to* **Polyneices'** *spirit.*

Antigone   He killed my Ety, I could never . . . But why? What happened to him?

Antigone *focuses on the crowd.*

Creon likes that you're not asking questions, 'cause the answers you find will change how you look at him. He wants you to forget the past, thinks it has no place in Britain. But it does. You have to acknowledge the past, *then* bury it, not leave it rotting in the air, pretending it doesn't exist.

What led Polyneices from one path to another? And the other six? When they asked for help, did we listen? They fell between the cracks, sons, daughters, leaders could fall too. We should try to bring them back. And if they die, the least we can do is bury them.

Chorus (*murmuring*)
   I guess so
   Never thought of it like that
   She's got a point.

Antigone   Creon says he is the head of families. Families look after their own right? But there's a dead son rotting in our living room. Creon's gone way off path.

Chorus (*murmuring*)
    He has you know
    He is proper lost
    She should do his job.

Nikomedes   She is doing it!

Antigone   I just wanted to bury my brother. What I did, I'd do again.

Creon *enters with the* **Commissioner**, **Aleksy** *and others.*

Creon   Who planned this?

Commissioner   I don't know.

Aleksy   Shut it down.

Chorus (*murmuring*)
    Let her go.
    Let her go!

Commissioner (*to* **Officers**)   Take her away. (*Whispering.*) But be gentle.

Chorus
    Let her go!
    Let her go!

Antigone   Because of this, I'm gonna be locked up?

Aleksy   Take her now or your head will roll!

Antigone   I buried my brother! Wouldn't you bury yours?

Chorus
    Let her go!
    Let her go!

Creon   Silence! SILENCE!

What the hell is this? Yes! I designed that law, to ensure that should you attack us, you won't just be stopped, you won't just be destroyed, your body will be left to rot.

Antigone   That's a person you're talking about.

Creon   You will be dumped in a courtyard for animals to scatter across the earth. Your soul will be restless and roam for eternity. This was the warning, the threat, the deterrent, and she has taken that from us.

Chorus *murmuring.*

Creon   She has swept the courtyard clean to welcome in our enemies, who will radicalise more young men, drive through more high streets, mowing down more of our families and children. This is what she has done, and you are making her the martyr Polyneices wishes he was.

Chorus
We're not doing that.
Are we?
I don't know.

Creon   You are continuing his work.

Chorus *murmuring.*

Antigone   After me, he will come for you!

Creon   My job is to make difficult decisions on your behalf, even if the decision affects me, my nephew, my niece, my son.

Antigone   Don't listen to him.

Creon   This is the real world, with clear and present dangers. This is what it means to love this country. I will protect you, whether you like it or not.

Antigone   This is not democratic.

Creon   You, I will make you an example the nation never forgets! The rest of you, go home! Return to the comfort I provide.

The crowd grumble and begin to disperse. The **Officer** *tries to lead* **Antigone** *away.* **Haemon** *tries to wrestle her free but is knocked to the ground.* **Aleksy** *pulls off* **Haemon**'s *disguise.*

Aleksy   You?!

Antigone   Haemon?! Did you set this up?

Haemon   No! I was trying to make them see / how wrong they were

Antigone   See what?! How the hell did you think this would help?

Creon   You! You are done!

Haemon   No. Dad let me / talk to her

Creon   Get her out! Leave! All of you.

Police *try to drag* **Antigone** *away.*

Antigone
 Lyra, is that you?
 Come back! Guys?! Athan, Strom!
 Fight back! Help me! Why aren't you helping?
 Come back! Come back! Please!

Police drag her away.

Scene Seven

A cross section of womxn in the city, including **Eurydice** *and* **Ismene***, are beside friends, lovers, husbands, wives, listening to* **Antigone**'s *voice across the airwaves.*

They read the speech from newspapers, point to it, sharing it with their companions.

Radio
 Aren't women attacked?
 Even by police?
 How many are killed by their partners each week?
 The world has a problem.
 It's men and power.

Eurydice

Don't ask if Antigone is right.
She was born in this city, she knows it at night.

Chorus

The nervous ways we walk the streets,
the many times I turn from men,
their prying eyes, their naked hunger.

They grope us in public, critique our bodies,
assault us in office, crush our dreams.

Not too long ago,
we weren't even allowed to vote.
Only men were citizens.
We spoke, but no one listening.

There are stories of fathers
who swapped their daughters
for farm utensils
and second-hand swords.

Others who buried
their daughters in shorts,
hoping next life,
they'd come back as boys.

The womxn, including **Kyria** *and* **Lyra** *begin to gather before*
Eurydice *and* **Ismene** *as* **Eurydice** *speaks.*

Eurydice

We flow from that dark history
and all men drink from its stream.
Only a few know it is poison,
most are in up to their knees.
The worst dive into its darkness,
drunk on how it makes them feel.

Ismene

And Creon has been touched by it.
I worked in his office. He crushed my dreams
of a fairer society, a better Britain

of individual liberty, tolerance, respect.
One person carries that torch today
they locked her up because she says
religion does not lead you astray,
your gender should not make you afraid,
respect our dead, there are no half-ways,
no clauses, no conditions!
Our society is full of dark traditions
she's saying those should change, not us!
They want to keep things as it is,
to silence Antigone.

Eurydice

Each of us, a drop of water,
we can form a mighty sea.
They think we're placid in this city,
puddles, lying amicably.

Ismene

Tonight, we're a walking wave
and Antigone must be freed.

They rally around **Ismene**. *She organises them into political
activists, all dressed in black.*

Scene Eight

Downing Street.

A lavish, reckless party. **Kyria** *and the* **Commissioner** *are there.*
Aleksy *wades through the guests to find* **Creon**.

Kyria   Prime Minister, that was exceptional, 'Return to the
comfort I provide.' So commanding, so powerful.

Aleksy   Sir.

Creon   I'm busy. Kyria, you were saying?

Aleksy   It is important.

Creon   Let it wait. Kyria?

Aleksy   It cannot. Tiresias is here.

Creon   Tiresias?

Beat.

Creon   Clear the room.

Commissioner   Sir?

Creon   Everyone, out.

Commissioner   I thought we could discuss curtailing the state of emergency?

Creon   NOW!

The **Commissioner** *clears the room.*

Creon   You too.

The **Commissioner** *exits. A female* **Bodyguard** *enters, followed by* **Tiresias***.*

Creon   Tiresias. It is unusual of you to come unannounced.

Tiresias   Creon. It is foolish of you to act without consultation.

Creon   Nothing required your counsel.

Tiresias   The country is split.

Aleksy   No. The data is clear, people across the country approve of him.

Tiresias   Data I provide. Correct? Your entire campaign ran on my advice. Was I ever incorrect?

Creon   No.

Tiresias   So you must listen and act accordingly.

Where I work, how I work is unfathomable to most. I have walls of super computers running simultaneous neural networks and simulations of every major city on Earth. I input into these every variable known to man. Traffic patterns, manufacturing trends, wind and rainfall, cotton harvests in the south, locust formations in the east, wage losses in ex-colonies, sectarian uprisings in the north. When an ant colony dies, there are ripple effects I can predict to the hour. I know about it, I log it, I plug it in. Do you follow me?

Creon   Yes.

Tiresias   Think of a spiderweb shaped as a cube. Imagine each silk strand of the web is every variable I input, radiating out of the cocoon. This is how I work. I enter into it. I swim within it. It swims within me. I glide through lines of code, riding algorithms of deep searches into pure data, like fish through water, like a consciousness through constellations, like eyes through stars. This country is my home. I know it in ways you cannot begin to imagine comprehending. Are you with me?

Creon   Yes.

Tiresias   Creon, you are balanced on a knife edge. Last night, I felt something. An old and unnatural disturbance.

A **Jinn** *appears, an abstraction of* **Polyneices'** *spirit, darker, mutilated.* **Tiresias** *is the only one who can sense this.*

Tiresias   I saw parts of it in the mouths of urban birds taking flight, rough foxes flocking around it, sprinting into the night, rats oozing up through it. It had a spirit that was there and not there, caught between worlds, a half formed thing, a ghost in my machine. I saw death, destruction, all you hold dear gone. It is coming. But you can stop it.

All men make mistakes, but a decent one admits his errors and makes amends. The only crime is pride. Bury the dead boy. Don't fight with a corpse. Where's the glory in that?

The **Jinn** *leaves.*

Aleksy   So even you have turned against him? He used to defend people like you, before it was fashionable, fought for your rights. Who paid you? How much?

Creon   For all the oil in the north, gold in the east, weapons in the west, diamonds in the south, I will not bury the terrorist.

Tiresias   Do you lack reason?

Creon   Do you lack loyalty? I am the Prime Minister.

Tiresias   Who made you Prime Minister?

Aleksy   I made him Prime Minister! Me. I hired you, and you sold me information you extracted, no, stole, from the public.

Tiresias   I provided a data service.

Aleksy   You created ways to manipulate people.

Tiresias   You could have used it for good, instead you targeted and lied, to everyone! You turned it into a weapon.

Aleksy   You built the weapon.

Tiresias   You pulled the trigger.

Aleksy   I'll expose you.

Tiresias   I'll expose you.

Aleksy   They'll hate you more than they'll hate me. There's a clarity to what I am. They understand me. But you shape shifting whatever the hell you are / they fear and do not

Tiresias   You snivelling bigot / I should never

Creon   Stop! Stop! Both of you!

What are you talking about? How do you work together?

Tiresias   I have a computer model of the British public. I ask this model questions, it spits out data I turn over to him.

Aleksy   And through analysis, my team and I translate the data into answers.

Beat.

Creon   Well, what's the problem?

Tiresias   It is my belief that he only utilises answers from certain subsections.

Aleksy   We targeted certain subsections to win the election.

Creon   Yes, but surely we are speaking to all sections now?

Aleksy   No. It's more economical not to.

Tiresias *laughs.*

Creon   It's more *economical*?

Aleksy   It's pointless asking some people somethings. Some people are irrelevant.

Beat.

Creon   Who decides who is irrelevant?

Aleksy   Pardon?

Creon   Who decides?

Aleksy   I do.

Tiresias *laughs.*

Beat.

Aleksy   Prime Minister, you are suggesting I lack objectivity?

Creon   You have an objective, Aleksy, you always do, it's your job!

Aleksy   This changes nothing.

Creon   How can you . . . don't you see / what this

Tiresias   He's not telling you everything, the destruction has started, Muslim businesses – corner shops are on fire.

Creon   Corner shops?

Tiresias   There's a 70 per cent rise in attacks against Muslims.

Creon   What?!

Aleksy   Those are not the votes that got you elected.

Creon   You knew about this? 70 per cent?!

Aleksy   A thousand or so attacks is an acceptable rise to stay in power.

Tiresias   Right wing groups are planning to *cleanse* the country, to disinfect / the city of

Aleksy   You, leave.

Tiresias   Creon, you still have time. Release the girl! Bury the boy!

Aleksy   Your contract is terminated.

Tiresias   Then LISTEN! You will pay for this, Creon. Not him, you. With blood! There are laws that govern worlds, analogue, digital and beyond, and what you've done cuts through all three. There are equations and old codes soldered into the firmaments of earth and you are messing with them. You've trapped who belongs to the next world in ours, and are forcing who belongs in ours to the next. You have stirred the guardian, that consuming ghost is hunting you. My systems are fried, I no longer have eyes, everything that happens next is on you. Women will march against you, all the wild dogs and vicious crows, low beasts and winged scavengers that feast on the dead will rise in our capital. Do what you want, I'm out.

Tiresias *and* **Bodyguard** *leave.*

Aleksy   They have gone, Sir.

Creon   Antigone . . . Polyneices . . .

Aleksy   We should hold our nerve.

Creon   Have they ever been wrong?

Aleksy   Who?

Creon   Tiresias! Who else?! Have they ever been wrong?

Aleksy   No.

Creon   Then we should at least reconsider.

Aleksy   To change your mind, in front of the country, the party, your enemies, there will be a vote of no confidence.

Creon   Women will march . . . an uprising?

Aleksy   Hold your nerve.

Creon   Was Antigone right? Have I underestimated the country? The British public?

Aleksy   The data proves / that the people

Creon   THE DATA?!

Aleksy   Regardless of data, draw from your experience. You know this country, what it is, who they are. You are after all a brown man . . .

Creon   Meaning?

Aleksy   The silent majority, all those knuckle dragging racists, you know what they think, what they want, what they fear.

Creon   And I played into that fear, made them fear us even more. Seventy per cent?! I'll pay for this with blood . . . Someone close to me will die!

Aleksy   The country comes first!

Creon   I am destroying the country!

Aleksy   Don't throw away everything I've worked for.

Creon   You've worked for?

Aleksy   I poured hours of myself into your campaign, I reshuffled the cabinet to give you absolute power.

Creon   Call the Commissioner.

Aleksy   No.

Creon   What?

Aleksy   You lacked confidence, conviction / clarity

Creon   You really think you made me?

Aleksy   My benefactors demanded I let you burn / but I told them

Creon   Benefactors?

Aleksy   You were an indecisive man. I moulded you into a leader. I know what's best for you.

Creon   This is what's best for me? In trying to protect the country, I've torn it apart. I did everything you . . . no, it was me. I did that. I did. With information from you . . . you knew and let it happen. My . . . family is falling apart / and

Aleksy   You've always been weak. I've been too soft on you.

Creon   I have no time for this.

Creon *takes out his phone.*

Creon   Get me the commissioner.

Aleksy *grabs* **Creon**'s *phone, smashes it. They fight.* **Creon** *knocks* **Aleksy** *down.*

Creon   You're fired! COMMISSIONER! COMMISSIONER!

The **Commissioner** *enters as* **Aleksy** *runs out.*

Creon   We have to release Antigone and bury Polyneices. Find Nikomedes, please do it now.

Creon *and* **Commissioner** *exit.* **Kyria** *appears, and calls* **Ismene**.

Kyria   Creon is making moves to Antigone.

Ismene   What's happening?

Kyria   I couldn't hear, but you should get there fast.

Ismene   Okay. The streets are filling up. We are on our way.

Scene Nine

Inside **Antigone***'s prison.*

Antigone *rips a pillow case into a make-shift hijab, wears it, lays a towel on the floor, and tries to pray, but cannot concentrate.*

After multiple attempts, she shouts . . .

Antigone   Arhhh!

She pulls down the hijab and covers her eyes with her palms, frustrated.

Nicey, I keep seeing you everywhere. Did I make a mistake when burying you? What do I need to do? I'll do anything.

Not sure what I can do, locked away from everyone, Lyra, Haemon . . . I don't know what's happening out there.

I wanna fix this, but I don't know how. I'd keep fighting but when or if I get out, they won't let me anywhere near my old life. The boys won't need me. They've . . . left me. What am I fighting for? God doesn't need my help. I could survive this, but I'd be surviving for the sake of surviving and that's not . . . And Creon wants to use me as an example? Of what? For what? I will not let them seem rot in here, day in day out, just to crawl out broken in years?! I will not give them the satisfaction! I will not be your prisoner! BRITAIN CAN FUC . . .

No, Ety died for this country, but it's lost its way. Maybe there's hope, but not from me, I'm done with that, I'm done with the dunya. They should be RIOTING OUT THERE! I . . . I can't sleep. Two, three hours tops, where I forget, then wake up and it breaks me again and again. I'm tired. I'm so tired. I just . . . miss Mum. Dad. I wish we could . . . I just . . . want . . . them to hold me again . . .

Eteocles *and* **Polyneices** *appear on stage.*

Antigone   Ety, Nicey, are you here?

You are waiting for me? Aren't you? For us to go together?

To go where none of this shit matters? To walk the path to
. . . God, to eternal peace, limitless serenity.

To remain here is to slow down my journey, our path . . . to
peace.

Ya Allah.

Forgive what I'm about to do, but accept me when I come
home.

Ash-Hadu An-la illaha illallah Wa ash-hadu anna
Muhammadun abduhu wa Rasoolu.

Okay. Chalo. Let's go.

Antigone *twirls the make-shift hijab into a kind of rope, looks into
the audience, then turns, walks upstage between her brothers, who
turn and follow her into the light.*

Scene Ten

Outside **Antigone**'s *prison.*

The womxn-led protesters arrive at the prison with **Haemon**
following. They carry flares, crowbars and megaphones. The **Guards**
struggle to control them.

Chorus
    Choose Love! Bury Hate! Free Free Antigone!
    Choose Love! Bury Hate! Free Free Antigone!

Creon *arrives with* **Nikomedes** *and the* **Commissioner**.

Chorus
    Boo! Free Free Antigone! Shame on you!
    Call yourself a leader? How d'you sleep at night?

Creon *struggles through them to get to the prison.*

Creon   OPEN THE GATES! OPEN THE GATES!
RELEASE ANTIGONE!

Creon *enters the prison but comes out carrying* **Antigone**, *dead.*
The **Chorus** *falls silent, shocked.*

Creon *lays her on the ground as* **Haemon** *and* **Ismene** *fall on*
their knees beside her.

Ismene   Antigone? Neenee? No!

Haemon   Dad, what have you done?

Creon! What have you done?

Haemon *pulls out a knife and runs at* **Creon**. *They fight,* **Creon**
wrestles away the knife and accidentally stabs **Haemon**. **Haemon**
falls.

Creon *drops the knife, bends to* **Haemon** *as* **Eurydice** *rushes to*
his side.

Creon   Haemon? Haemon?

Haemon   My son! My son! He is dead. He is dead.

Eurydice *runs at* **Creon**, *pounding him.*

Eurydice   I warned you! I warned you!

The **Commissioner** *pulls her away.*

Nikomedes   Nothing is fixed. Nothing is permanent,
nothing on Allah's Earth will last for ever. May he have
mercy.

Ismene *rises to her feet.*

Ismene   Nikomedes, we need you.

Nikomedes   I can't take anymore.

Creon   Ismene

Ismene   Don't touch me!

Creon   Is this Allah? Is this punishment? Is this the
destroyer? I can't . . . I'm drowning, something is crushing
me. Compassionate, merciful Allah, take me. Take me now.

The **Public** *appear as* **Chorus**.

Chorus
   Remember those days of battle and brawn
   when the soul of the country was scattered and torn
   and the throne of power was empty and none
   of the candidates clamouring was clearly the one?

   Before he could torch our homes and towers
   destroy us, crush us completely,
   our great city which never cowers,
   rose up before him, brave shouting Freeze!

   My sister now, always keeps schtum,
   sits in her classroom sucking her thumb
   to keep a low profile, acts like she's dumb
   she's now a ghost of the star that she was

   She came in the night, she gazed at the world,
   and the light of her eyes was a righteous sword.
   She gathered her wings and entered the darkness
   and knelt by her love and set her love free.

   Aren't women attacked too?
   Even by police?
   How many are killed
   by partners each week?

   What if there was silence
   and we published . . . air?
   What might fill the quiet?
   What is there that's rare?

Ismene   Nikomedes, you will come to bury my sister.
I have to do her honour, I am the last one.
The questions she asked grow louder now she's gone.
We must answer all of them, every last one.

End of play.

Black out.

For a complete listing of
Methuen Drama titles, visit:
www.bloomsbury.com/drama

Follow us on Twitter and keep up to date
with our news and publications
@MethuenDrama